PERSONAL PERFORMANCE CONTRACTS:

Setting Realistic Goals

REVISED EDITION

Roger Fritz

A FIFTY-MINUTE™ SERIES BOOK

CRISP PUBLICATIONS, INC.
Menlo Park, California

PERSONAL PERFORMANCE CONTRACTS:
Setting Realistic Goals

REVISED EDITION

Roger Fritz

CREDITS
Editor: **Michael Crisp**
Layout and Composition: **Interface Studio**
Cover Design: **Carol Harris**

Copyright © 1987, 1993 by Crisp Publications, Inc.
Printed in the United States of America

English language Crisp books are distributed worldwide. Our major international distributors include:

CANADA: Reid Publishing, Ltd., Box 69559—109 Thomas St., Oakville, Ontario Canada L6J 7R4. TEL: (416) 842-4428, FAX: (416) 842-9327

AUSTRALIA: Career Builders, P. O. Box 1051, Springwood, Brisbane, Queensland, Australia 4127. TEL: 841-1061, FAX: 841-1580

NEW ZEALAND: Career Builders, P. O. Box 571, Manurewa, Auckland, New Zealand. TEL: 266-5276, FAX: 266-4152

JAPAN: Phoenix Associates Co., Mizuho Bldg. 2-12-2, Kami Osaki, Shinagawa-Ku, Tokyo 141, Japan. TEL: 3-443-7231, FAX: 3-443-7640

Selected Crisp titles are also available in other languages. Contact International Rights Manager Tim Polk at (800) 442-7477 for more information.

Library of Congress Catalog Card Number 92-073961
Fritz, Roger
Personal Performance Contracts
ISBN 1-56052-197-X

This book is printed on recyclable paper with soy ink.

FOR KATE — WHO ACCEPTED
THE BEST CONTRACT I EVER MADE

ACKNOWLEDGEMENTS

One of my major objectives in preparing this revision was to include a sample Performance Contract for a variety of jobs. I am especially grateful for the help received from the following people, each of whom are leaders in their field.

Jon Helwig—V.P. Information Services, Brookfield, Inc.

Katherine Holliman—Personnel Director, Tulane University Hospital/Clinics

Steve Johnson—Partner, Schillerstrom & Kabza Accountants

Scott Lehman—Director of Operations, Pizza Huts of Cincinnati, Inc.

Becky Mangus—Realtor, Coldwell Banker

Rocky Rockett—Vice President of Client Services, Resource Information Management Systems, Inc.

Joe Terrell—Director of Human Resources, Famous Footwear

ABOUT THIS BOOK

Personal Performance Contracts: Setting Realistic Goals is not like most books. It has a unique ''self-paced'' format that encourages a reader to become personally involved. Designed to be ''read with a pencil,'' there is an abundance of exercises, activities, assessments and cases that invite participation.

The objective of *Personal Performance Contracts* is to help a manager learn what a Personal Performance Contract is; why it is a fundamental skill of management; and how to complete one in a professional manner. Managers can then make any required behavioral changes applying concepts presented in the book to their unique management situation.

Personal Performance Contracts (and the other self-improvement books listed on page 93) can be used effectively in a number of ways. Here are some possibilities:

— Individual Study. Because the book is self-instructional, all that is needed is a quiet place, some time and a pencil. By completing the activities and exercises, a manager should not only receive valuable feedback, but also practical ideas about steps for self-improvement.

— Workshops and Seminars. The book is ideal for pre-assigned reading prior to a workshop or seminar. With the basics in hand, the quality of the participation should improve. More time can be spent on concept extensions and applications during the program. The book can also be effective when a trainer distributes it at the beginning of a session, and leads participants through the contents.

— Remote Location Training. Copies can be sent to those not able to attend ''home office'' training sessions.

There are other possibilities that depend on the objectives, program or ideas of the user. One thing's for sure—even after it has been read, this book will serve as excellent reference material which can be easily reviewed. Good luck!

TO THE MANAGER OR TRAINER—

Personal Perfromance Contracts has been prepared to meet two needs: (1) Self study, and (2) Group training. The ideas presented in this book are workable; and the methods recommended have been proven on the job.

For group training the following is recommended:

Introduce and discuss, ''Where Are You Now?,''
   pp. 2-10, first hour.
Introduce and discuss, ''Preparing the Performance Contract,''
   pp. 11-28, one hour.
Introduce and discuss, ''Action Needed to Produce Results,''
   pp. 29-53, one hour.
Discuss, ''Introducing the Personal Performance Contract,''
   pp. 54-66, one hour.
Discuss the step-by-step process,
   pp. 67-76, one hour.
Critique ''Your Personal Performance Contract,''
   p. 79, one hour.

The six hours of training can be accomplished in a single day (with breaks at mid-morning, mid-afternoon, and lunch), or done effectively in two half-day sessions.

The essence of the Personal Performance Contract is a recorded agreement between individuals. Each person should feel ''ownership'' in an agreement before any written document is made final.

During group training it is recommended that the trainer spend time with each individual in order to maximize the benefits.

Remember—good intentions are not enough. Lasting improvement comes only when we know what is expected and deliberately set a course to achieve it. A Personal Performance Contract is the most simple and direct way to give meaning to personal goals and accomplish company priorities. This means employees must be active participants. Once this has been accomplished the benefits will repay your efforts to implement PPCs many times over.

—Roger Fritz

TO THE READER—

"If you don't know where you're going, any road will take you there!"

How important is performance to you? To your organization?

This book deals with the basic essentials of achieving success at work. Success has nothing to do with luck, or being at the right place at the right time, or knowing the right person. These can help but success is achieved by those who know how to prepare for it. At work this means a deliberate method of determining who will do what by when.

Personal Performance Contracts sets the stage for performance. It enables supervisors and employees to prepare jointly and commit to agreements. Performance Contracts cement job commitments. Once parties become obligated to each other, performance should improve because accountability has been established and agreed upon.

My objective will have been met when you put the simple and direct principles in this book to work for you.

—Roger Fritz

The most important question for all employers, at all times, under all circumstances is—What do we mean by performance?

CONTENTS

CONTENTS

Regardless of your experience as a supervisor or manager, it is important that you know what Personal Performance Contracts are; why they are important; and how to construct one that will achieve significant results. This book will help you accomplish these objectives. For openers, it is important to discover where you are now.

GETTING
STARTED

WHERE ARE YOU NOW?

Here are some important questions to determine where you are now.
Answer each question honestly:

DO YOU CURRENTLY HAVE SPECIFIC WRITTEN PERFORMANCE
GOALS OR STANDARDS AGAINST WHICH YOUR ACHIEVEMENT
CAN BE MEASURED?

(　)　YES　　　(　)　NO

DO YOUR SUPERVISOR/EMPLOYEES KNOW ABOUT THEM?

(　)　YES　　　(　)　NO

DO YOU REGULARLY RECONFIRM YOUR GOALS AND STANDARDS
IN ORDER TO REMAIN ON TARGET?

(　)　YES　　　(　)　NO

ARE YOUR ON-THE-JOB GOALS SUFFICIENTLY FLEXIBLE TO MEET NEW
DEMANDS OR UNEXPECTED CHANGES IN THE DIRECTION
OF WORK?

(　)　YES　　　(　)　NO

ARE YOU BASICALLY SATISFIED THAT YOU AND/OR YOUR PEOPLE
ARE MAKING MEASURABLE PROGRESS TOWARD ESTABLISHED
WORK GOALS?

(　)　YES　　　(　)　NO

IS IT LIKELY YOUR SUPERIORS/SUBORDINATES WOULD AGREE
THAT YOU ARE ACCURATELY EVALUATING PROGRESS TOWARD
YOUR GOALS?

(　)　YES　　　(　)　NO

ARE YOU CONFIDENT THAT ACHIEVING YOUR GOALS WILL BE
REWARDED FAIRLY?

(　)　YES　　　(　)　NO

<u>Regardless of How You Answered the Questions on Page 3:</u>

You should realize that performance goals aren't about run-of-the-mill daily chores. They're expected. They keep the engine running. But their top speed is only second gear.

Performance goals discussed in this book must meet certain criteria. They must:

* Be important enough to create some excitement or enthusiasm and stimulate extra effort.

* Be challenging enough so results will bring rewards that outweigh the effort required to achieve them.

* Cover a long enough time to accommodate short-range setbacks and disappointments

> The best method for achieving outstanding performance, meeting objectives and insuring appropriate recognition is to prepare and use PERSONAL PERFORMANCE CONTRACTS!

PERSONAL PERFORMANCE CONTRACTS: A DEFINITION

WHAT IS A PERSONAL PERFORMANCE CONTRACT? (PPC)

In simplest terms, a PERSONAL PERFORMANCE CONTRACT is a **WRITTEN AGREEMENT** between an employee and his or her manager which **RECORDS ACCOMPLISHMENTS** to be achieved within a **SPECIFIC TIME PERIOD**. Accomplishments should have **BENEFITS** for the employee as well as for the organization.

Here are the basic steps to be taken when constructing a PPC agreement:

1. Engage in a careful job **analysis** to pinpoint the most important needs which are to be satisfied.

2. Prepare **objectives** for the highest priority needs identified in the analysis. Achievement of these objectives should be vital to success on that job.

3. Develop an **action plan** which specifies exactly who will be doing what by when.

4. Prepare a **time & cost schedule** to measure accurately the dollar impact of achievement within a specific time frame.

5. Emphasize **self-development** as an integral part of the agreement.

6. Conduct regular **reviews** to ensure progress meets expectations.

This description is equally true for your Personal Performance Contract as well as those who report to you.

Preparing and implementing an effective Performance Contract is never a routine chore–even for experienced people. It demands commitment, but also offers these significant benefits:

1. A unique opportunity to view the job from two important viewpoints–that of the boss <u>and</u> the employee.

2. A method by which to agree on needs and identify priorities.

3. A format that allows continual concentration on objectives.

4. A chance for the employee to see the "big picture," and better understand any changes that occur.

5. A clearer focus on those problems and/or obstacles that require a solution.

6. A means to pinpoint accountability for action (<u>who</u> will do <u>what</u> by <u>when</u>?).

(THE NEXT PAGE MAY BE REPRODUCED WITHOUT PRIOR PERMISSION. COPIES SHOULD BE GIVEN TO EACH PERSON FOR COMPLETION.)

SUCCESS DEFINED*

Complete the following activity. Prepare as complete a list as possible. See the next page for a comparison of ideas.

A SUCCESSFUL EMPLOYEE IS ONE WHO:

SUCCESS FOR ME PERSONALLY MEANS:

SUCCESS IN MY JOB DEPENDS ON MY ABILITY TO:

MY FORMULA FOR ACHIEVING SUCCESS IS:

*Ask those preparing a PPC to complete this page.

Definitions of success will be as different as the number of people involved. Successful people, however, have several common characteristics. These include:

* An ability to stand on one's own feet.

* Courage to assume responsibility for decisions that are made.

* The ability to set some personal development goals.

* A willingness to pursue what is "right" versus what is easy, quick or popular.

Successful people also understand that growth is natural and change is part of growth.

Ask those who work with you to consider things about themselves that are truly unique, those skills and characteristics that make them feel confident and proficient. Then ask them to consider how they can best apply their talents.

EVALUATING STRENGTHS*

Answer each of the following questions as honestly as you can.

1. MOST ASPECTS OF MY JOB REALLY TURN ME ON.

    (   ) YES   (   ) NO

2. I HAVE PERSONAL GROWTH OBJECTIVES THAT ARE CLEAR TO ME.

    (   ) YES   (   ) NO

3. THE CONTRIBUTIONS I MAKE ARE VALUED BY MY EMPLOYER.

    (   ) YES   (   ) NO

4. I AM WILLING TO ACCEPT ACCOUNTABILITY AND RESPONSIBILITY
    FOR MY JOB ACTIONS AND DECISIONS.

    (   ) YES   (   ) NO

5. I HAVE LEARNED FROM PAST MISTAKES AND FAILURES.

    (   ) YES   (   ) NO

6. I BELIEVE I AM MAKING FULL USE OF MY KNOWLEDGE AND
    EXPERIENCE WHILE ON THE JOB.

    (   ) YES   (   ) NO

NOW TURN THE PAGE AND COMPARE YOUR ANSWERS. BE SURE YOUR
EMPLOYEES ALSO COMPLETE THIS EXERCISE AND REVIEW THEIR
ANSWERS WITH THEM INDIVIDUALLY.

*Ask those preparing a PPC to complete this page.

10

AUTHOR'S RESPONSE

1. IF YOU ANSWERED "NO," take a hard look at your job. You might be happier in another position. If you basically like what you do, try handling some of your routines in a new, more creative way. Test your originality. Read for new ideas. Talk with colleagues on ways they stay motivated. Experiment for better results.

2. IF YOU ANSWERED "YES," you have discovered that the key to success lies in creating meaningful targets to shoot for, and that satisfaction comes when these targets are achieved.

3. IF YOUR ANSWER WAS "NO," ask yourself if you are utilizing all the knowledge, skills and experience garnered over the years. How do you view the potential within your current job? How about your boss? Do you get enough feedback from her or him on the value of your contributions?

4. IF YOU CHECKED "YES" to this question, congratulations! It's obvious you have self-confidence. You also probably recognize that everyone has moments when they feel inadequate. You understand that risking a mistake is better than doing nothing.

5. IF YOU ANSWERED "NO," you have missed a great learning experience. Disappointments should not defeat you. Study your mistakes to avoid similar problems in the future. Maintain an optimistic outlook. Failures have a way of stretching your abilities. Remember: Avoiding failure is not the same as success!

6. A "NO" ANSWER SUGGESTS you may not have clearly defined what is essential to your advancement. Do you resist change or use it as a step forward? Are you committed to an ideal? An action? A challenge?

10

KEYS TO JOB SUCCESS

The previous exercise should suggest existing opportunities you and/or your people may have overlooked. Certainly what has been revealed indicates an opening for a more creative use of talent.

Successful people in business are motivated by many things. We all can identify money, status or power, but none of these are as important as satisfaction. Truly successful people are determined to do a good job, make a contribution, or advance their business or profession for the personal satisfaction that comes from a job well done.

THE KEY TO JOB SUCCESS LIES IN A PLANNED, SUSTAINED EFFORT. THE BEST WAY TO ENSURE THIS SUCCESS IS WITH A CAREFULLY-THOUGHT-OUT PERFORMANCE CONTRACT BETWEEN YOU AND YOUR BOSS—AS WELL AS BETWEEN YOU AND THE PEOPLE WHO REPORT TO YOU.

The balance of this book will explain how to develop a practical and realistic Personal Performance Contract.

CASE STUDIES

Case studies provide insights about the content being introduced.

The first case (on the facing page) can help you better understand the importance of reviewing job requirements before beginning the PPC process.

CASE 1

CASE 1: DIFFICULT CHOICES

Harry Phillips just completed his first year as Manager. He is a good performer, but he occasionally has problems dealing with people. He supervises six people, most of whom had been peers. One of his subordinates, Production Supervisor Joe Jefferson, is four years from retirement. Joe is in good health, competent and friendly, but works at a very relaxed pace. Harry had done little about this because he had no clear-cut idea about how to motivate Joe. In fact, Harry has found the situation embarrassing because, although he likes supervising, he hates dealing with problems like Joe's lack of productivity. It is hard for him to accept that he has a tendency to avoid these problems rather than face them.

Another problem in Harry's department is Jim Thomas, his Engineering Supervisor. Jim is about Harry's age. Everyone knows that Jim wanted the job Harry received. Jim felt he deserved the advancement instead of Harry. Since Harry's promotion, Jim has been polite when dealing with Harry, but his work has fallen off significantly both in quantity and quality. Harry had not talked to Jim about this, even though it is noticeable to everyone. It seems to Harry that the problem is getting worse because the two young engineers who work with Jim are also slacking off. The younger men complain frequently to Harry about how little Joe and Jim are accomplishing.

A. How could a Personal Performance Contract help Harry deal with Joe and Jim?

B. What key result areas should Joe's personal PPC include?

C. What key result areas should Jim's PPC include?

D. How much time would you allow for the benefits of the PPC to become evident?

(See Author's responses on page 83).

PREPARING THE PERFORMANCE CONTRACT

A recent study conducted by industrial psychologists summarized the attitudes of over 200,000 employees toward their companies.

The results?

More than half took a dim view of their workplace and their company.

A majority resented the way layoffs were handled.

Most felt there was too great a difference in pay between supervisors and those supervised.

Almost half questioned the integrity of management.

Sixty percent lacked confidence in their company's future.

Most worried because they had so little say about decisions which affected their future.

DO YOUR EMPLOYEES...

UNDERSTAND conditions faced by your company in the marketplace, including the strength of competitors and the resulting effect on company policies and procedures?

DEVELOP specific, achievable, realistic objectives for their own jobs— objectives that can measurably move the company forward?

PREPARE action plans to ensure the kind of consistent results required for success?

REMAIN alert for problems and obstacles that need to be resolved or eliminated before progress can be made?

RELATE their personal performance to objectives that the company expects to accomplish?

THE COMMON DENOMINATOR OF ALL THESE ISSUES IS THE FOUNDATION OF THE PERSONAL PERFORMANCE CONTRACT! Your first step is on the next page.

STEP 1

COMPLETE A JOB ANALYSIS WORKSHEET

Employees need to understand their jobs and where they are headed before good decisions can be made. Like taking a trip, you must know where you are going before you decide how to prepare for your journey and how to get on the right road.

To conduct a realistic evaluation of your present situation involves similar planning. You must ORGANIZE FACTS AND DETERMINE POSSIBLE COURSES OF ACTION.

To do this, you (and/or your employees) should complete a job analysis worksheet similar to the one on the following page. It will help answer questions such as:

* Is the information about my job accurate and complete?

* Do I have a current job description or set of job objectives?

* Have I prioritized the key results expected in order to concentrate on items that deserve the most attention?

* Am I aware of any trends that may require changes in procedure, or indicate a potential danger.

* Have I considered new ways to approach my job that can save time, effort and/or money?

HERE ARE SOME OF THE MORE PRODUCTIVE INFORMATION SOURCES FOR YOU AND/OR YOUR EMPLOYEES.

* Past Performance Appraisals

* Key memos/letters/directives

* Pertinent company reports

* Quotas/budgets/forecasts

* Job-related coaching/counseling/training sessions

* Direct observation of behavior

ADD ANY ADDITIONAL SOURCES THAT COULD BE USEFUL.

JOB ANALYSIS WORKSHEET*

CHECKPOINTS	FACTS/INFORMATION AFFECTING JOB PERFORMANCE	TIMING/IDEAS/ SUGGESTIONS TO INCLUDE IN CONTRACT
JOB PURPOSE What is the major purpose of my job? • What KNOWLEDGE is required? (marketing, customers, economics, etc.) • What SKILLS are necessary? (problem solving, writing, decision making, salesmanship, etc.) • What TRAITS are needed? (self-confidence, empathy, aggressiveness, etc.) What was I REALLY hired to accomplish? Do I have a true sense of the way things WORK in this company? What RESOURCES from the company are available to me? Am I taking full advantage of them? RESPONSIBILITIES In what areas am I STRONGEST? WEAKEST? How well do I organize my TIME? DUTIES? Other job ACTIVITIES? PERFORMANCE Do I know what PRIORITIES are most important to the company? How well do I IMPLEMENT them?	EDUCATION/EXPERIENCE What can I offer in the way of education/experience/expertise not now available from other people in the company? COMMUNICATION SKILLS How well do I communicate to subordinates? Peers? Supervisors? Other departments? COOPERATION What degree of rapport have I established with other departments within the company? BIG PICTURE Am I aware of key company priorities? How well do I help implement them? PAST PERFORMANCE How do those with whom I work feel about my job performance? What about supervisors? Peers? BUDGET ANALYSIS Am I able to keep operating costs within budget? Have I pointed out areas to my supervisor in which savings are possible?	When and under what circumstances should the contract be presented? Does information in the contract answer most of the questions my boss is likely to ask? What parts of the contract should be communicated to my peers? Subordinates? Others? Have all explanations been presented for additional costs, or other changes to the current work environment?

(USE THE BLANK WORKSHEET ON THE NEXT PAGES TO DO YOUR OWN JOB ANALYSIS.)

JOB ANALYSIS WORKSHEET*

CHECKPOINTS	FACTS/INFORMATION AFFECTING JOB PERFORMANCE	TIMING/IDEAS/ SUGGESTIONS TO INCLUDE IN CONTRACT
<u>JOB PURPOSE</u>		
<u>RESPONSIBILITIES</u>		
<u>PERFORMANCE</u>		

*This sheet may be reproduced without permission of the publisher.

JOB ANALYSIS WORKSHEET*

CHECKPOINTS	FACTS/INFORMATION AFFECTING JOB PERFORMANCE	TIMING/IDEAS/ SUGGESTIONS TO INCLUDE IN CONTRACT
JOB PURPOSE		
RESPONSIBILITIES		
PERFORMANCE		

*This sheet may be reproduced without permission of the publisher.

STEP 2 | SELECT PRIORITY OBJECTIVES

A careful look at the Job Analysis Worksheet just completed should help identify the highest priority goals to use in your performance contract.

The three basic categories of performance are:

1. <u>Job Routines</u> that need improvement. (Daily chores such as preparation of reports; customer service; quality control; training, etc.). Although "routine" they are too important to be considered trivial. They are the lubricant that keep the business functioning smoothly. When the basics are understood and controlled more important new objectives can be pursued.

2. <u>Problems That Need To Be Solved</u>. People who learn to become problem solvers have special value to their organizations. Problem solvers resolve a lack of progress by taking a results-oriented approach.

3. <u>Innovations For Added Benefits</u>. Those capable of providing true job innovations are the "champions." This special group takes positive action that provides creative breakthroughs.

INDIVIDUAL AND ORGANIZATION OBJECTIVES

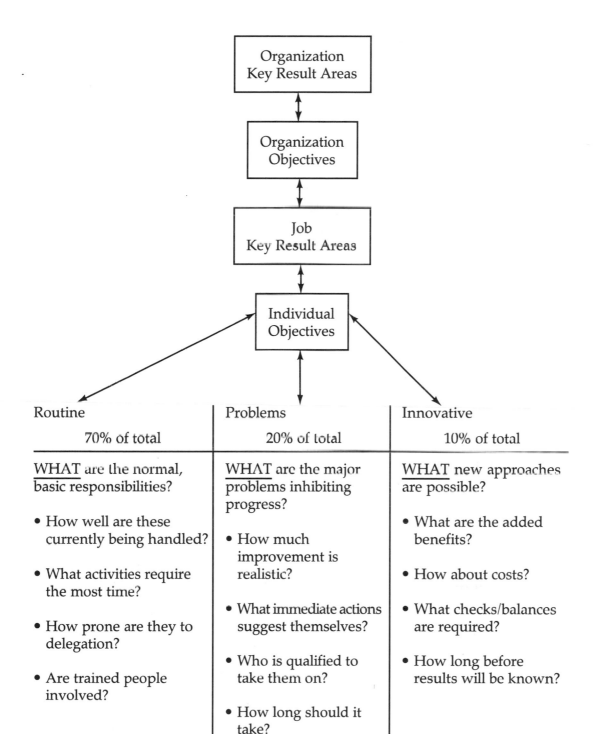

Routine	Problems	Innovative
70% of total	20% of total	10% of total
<u>WHAT</u> are the normal, basic responsibilities?	<u>WHAT</u> are the major problems inhibiting progress?	<u>WHAT</u> new approaches are possible?
• How well are these currently being handled?	• How much improvement is realistic?	• What are the added benefits?
• What activities require the most time?	• What immediate actions suggest themselves?	• How about costs?
• How prone are they to delegation?	• Who is qualified to take them on?	• What checks/balances are required?
• Are trained people involved?	• How long should it take?	• How long before results will be known?

THREE IMPORTANT CRITERIA

The priority objectives you select (page 20) should meet three criteria. They must be:

1. <u>REASONABLE:</u>
   - Can they be achieved in the time available?

   - Will they bring about desired changes?

   - Will costs be within allowable budgets?

   - Will they create new problems?

2. <u>SPECIFIC:</u>
   - Do they specify what the improvements will be?

   - Do they explain when results can be expected?

3. <u>AMBITIOUS:</u>
   - Are they sufficiently challenging and rewarding?

   - Will they resolve problems and/or seize new opportunities?

   - If implemented, will they be profitable?

THE CONCEPT OF KEY RESULT AREAS

What is a Key Result Area?

A prevailing attitude among those who hesitate to commit themselves to performance contracts is the belief that it is not possible to measure the work they perform. This is heard more frequently from those who deal with intangibles, such as values, or services, as compared to those whose jobs involve manufactured items, or sales quotas.

Some jobs are more difficult to measure than others, but none are impossible to measure. The problem is reduced greatly when a job is broken into its component parts. Separate responsibilities or duties can be itemized. These distinct job parts are called key result areas. They are not goals, but areas of responsibility from which specific goals can be prepared. A key result area answers the questions: ''What are the things I am accountable for?'' ''What are the major component parts of my job?''

For example:

KEY RESULT AREA FOR BILL JONES

1. Responsible for all production schedules

2. Responsible for finished product quality control

3. Responsible for safety in production department

4.

PRIMARY NEEDS BY KEY RESULT AREA

1. Back order delays are causing some loss of customer business

2. Quality has fallen below the 96% acceptable target

3. Lost time due to accidents has increased 8% during past 6 months

4.

24

The best way to eliminate disagreement and conflict over what was accomplished is to determine in advance how progress will be measured. Indicators are best expressed in terms of Quality, Quantity, Time and Cost.

HOW CAN PROGRESS
BE MEASURED?

(Examples of Progress Indicators)

QUANTITY	Number of customers/clients served per month...quarter...etc.
	Number items processed (orders, forms) per week...month...etc.
	Average backlog of orders per day...month...etc.
	Number cases handled (referrals, complaints) per quarter...etc.
	Number of customer complaints per year...etc.
	% employee participation (in specific programs)
	Number person hours lost to absenteeism per quarter...etc.
QUALITY	Error rate/ratio (by department...project...etc.)
	Production hours lost due to injury (severity rate) per quarter...year...etc.
	% orders without error
	Rate of employee turnover
	% tests repeated
	% work redone (or rejected completely)
	% time out of order (downtime) or unproductive
TIME	# or % deadlines missed
	# or % answered within 5 days
	# of days to complete
	# of working days after end of month/quarter
	Time elapsed (turn-around time)
	Frequency each month/quarter
COST	% variance from budget
	$ as line item in budget (e.g., overtime)
	Dollars saved over previous period/quarter
	$ cost per person contact or order received
	# hours to complete each time

Use the sample worksheet on the next page as a guide.

Progress Indicator Worksheet for Betsy Stevens, Production Supervisor

KEY RESULT AREA	% Importance	Measures Quantity/Quality/Time/Cost
Cost Control	25%	# written bid specifications? % competitive bids on components? deadline met for 3% expense reduction? stayed within total budget?
Production Scheduling	40%	# or % schedules met? # or % on-time shipments? deadlines missed by product?

Quality Control	20%	$ value of wasted material?
		$ value of product recalled?
		# or type of customer complaints?

Safety	15%	# accidents? classified by severity? downtown? insurance costs?
	100%	

NOW YOU TRY IT

Progress Indicators Worksheet* for _____

Name

KEY RESULT AREA	% Importance	Measures Quantity/Quality/Time/Cost
	100%	

*This sheet may be copied without further permission of the publisher.

28

KEY QUESTIONS

After determining the key result areas (normally 4 or 5 for each job), and the most important current need for each area (review page 23), the next step is to schedule a meeting to ensure there is agreement between an employee and his/her manager on questions such as:

- Why are listed needs important?

- What key results are expected?

- What are the potential obstacles?

- What is the organization's performance target?

- How will progress be measured in terms of quality, quantity, time & cost?

- What is the action plan for accountability–<u>who</u> will be doing <u>what</u> by <u>when</u>?

The following pages show samples of how a personal performance analysis will lead from the general to the specific as each question is answered.

A variety of 10 widely-held jobs is provided to allow maximum opportunity for you to compare with your situation.

SAMPLE

PERSONAL PERFORMANCE CONTRACT WORKSHEET

For: **Manufacturing**

Key Result Area	Need	Why Important	How Important %	Potential Obstacles	Performance Targets/Results Expected	Measures Quality/Quantity Time, Cost	Action Plan (Who, What, When)
Cost Control	Reduce departmental expenses by 15% during 2nd quarter	Profits must be improved	25%	Vendor prices too high & competition limited	Bid costs on all components — Locate minimum of three new suppliers	% improvement upon completion	Jim T. propose bid specs by 4/10 John T. Approve by 4/15 Frank O. implement by 5/20
Production Scheduling	Reduce backorder delays to 3 work days	Losing key customers	40%	Cost of new equipment Employee resistance	Automate component assembly on line 1 & 2 by 9/1	Deadline missed by product % customers retained Startup date met?	Jane N.—prepare report by 5/1 Max R.—approve plan by 5/12 Joe P.—complete automation project by 6/30
Supplies	Stock outages delaying shipments	Lost 4 customers last month with total orders of $185,000	15%	Unreliable vendors No inspections in receiving dept.	Get new vendors Assign inspector to receiving dept.	# days to complete # customers regained % shipment rejected $ value of shipments delayed	Nancy G.—get new vendor by 4/20 Tom H.—select and train new inspector by 4/30
Security	Eliminate employee theft	Inventory loss was $55,000 last quarter	10%	Most material is in unrestricted storage areas	Reduce inventory loss by 50% in 3 months	# incidents of theft $ amount of missing material	Susan M.—recommend action by 4/1 Jack C.—provide locked storage for priority materials by 4/15
Safety	Lost time due to accidents up 30% in 1st Qtr.	Insurance costs up 60% in past 2 years Paid time off increasing	10%	Finding a new insurance carrier Supervisors are indifferent	Reduce frequency rate by 10% this quarter Reduce severity rate by 12% this quarter	# & % of incident reports prepared next day Manhours lost Cost to correct unsafe conditions	Leslie B.—prepare weekly report beginning 4/1 Mark D.—recommend corrective action by 5/1 Sam S.—implement by 6/30
			100%				

This contract is for the period _____ to _____ .
(mth/day/yr)   (mth/day/yr)

Signed _____   Signed _____
                                                                (supervisor)

SAMPLE

PERSONAL PERFORMANCE CONTRACT WORKSHEET

For: **Registered Nurse**

Key Result Area	Need	Why Important	How Important %	Potential Obstacles	Performance Targets/Results Expected	Measures Quality/Quantity Time, Cost	Action Plan (Who, What, When)
Patient Assessment	Accurate information • Upon admission • Beginning of each shift	• Anticipate needs—Set up treatment • Basis to monitor treatment	10%	• High case load • Understaffed	• Perform assessment within 2 hours of admission • Head to toe exam at start of each shift	• On time • Accuracy	*Jane N.* Daily document assessments accurately and completely
Planning	• Document potential problems • Institute discharge plan to limit length of stay	Keep costs as low as possible	15%	Doctors unavailable	Review/revise care plan every 8 hours	Weekly discharge planning rounds	*Sue K.* Addresses patient/family teaching in plan of care *Marge B.* Complete discharge planning form
Patient Care Plan Implementation	• Organize time based on current patient needs • Document care given	• Alter treatment as need arises • Record charges • Provide completely accurate reports for physicians and nursing staff	40%	• Many emergency situations • Changes in work load	Provide accurate documentation for patient recovery and family education	Review patient records every 2 hours and at the end of the shift	*Pat S.* Communicates patient status to on-coming shift and physician(s) *Denise R.* Distribute educational material to patient/family
Patient Evaluation	Accurately diagnose patient progress and prescribe post-discharge actions	Recovery at optimum pace	10%	Poor communication between shifts	Evaluate and document plan of care and patient/family response	Continuing accurate documentation	*Duty Nurse* • Make patient rounds every 2 hours • Document outcome every 2 hours

Key Result Area	Need	Why Important	How Important %	Potential Obstacles	Performance Targets/Results Expected	Measures Quality/Quantity Time, Cost	Action Plan (Who, What, When)
Customer Relations	Provide current accurate information on patient status	Meet reasonable expectation of patient and family	10%	• East to defer • Emergencies interfere	Daily briefing for patient and/or designated family member	Consistently ranks above 90% on patient surveys	*Staff Nurse* Records all briefings *Department Head* Conducts monthly feedback seminar sessions for all staff
Professional and Staff Development	Professional growth	Awareness of new procedures and improvement programs	5%	Scheduling staff to be available for conferences while keeping areas staffed	• Monitor learning needs quarterly • Complete programs agreed upon	Participate in 2 Quality Improvement programs this quarter	*Dept. Head and each Staff Nurse* • will begin on 8/1 Laura R. • will complete first unit by 5/15 and second unit by 6/30
Safety	Lost time accidents too high	Must meet accreditation standards	5%	Unbudgeted expense for new equipment	Maintain compliance with National standards	Correctly utilizes occurrence reports	*Staff Nurse* • Check code cart as assigned • Pass test on safety manuals by 2/1
Leadership	Initiate and coordinate action on patients behalf	• Patients expect it • Eliminate delays	5%	• "Turf protection' • Doctors not available	Daily assignment of shift "group leader"	No unresolved decisions at end of shift	*Dept. Head* • Makes assignments 24 hours in advance • Send daily reports of unresolved issues to Medical Director

This contract is for the period _____ to _____
(mth/day/yr)   (mth/day/yr)

Signed _____

Signed _____
(supervisor)

Personal Performance Contracts

SAMPLE

PERSONAL PERFORMANCE CONTRACT WORKSHEET

For: **Secretary**

Key Result Area	Need	Why Important	How Important %	Potential Obstacles	Performance Targets/Results Expected	Measures Quality/Quantity Time, Cost	Action Plan (Who, What, When)
Typing and Word Processing	Improve productivity	Costs must be reduced	40%	Equipment outdated	Increase average words per minute	By 15% with 100% accuracy within 6 month	Gloria C. will train entire staff week of 9/15
Transcribing Dictation	Saves time for managers	Provides flexibility for managers	20%	Too many tapes are garbled	• Train all managers • Increase words per minute	• Use new training program provided by vendor • By 20% with 95% accuracy within 6 months	• Joe P. will conduct by 7/25 • Ellen W. will critique sample output of all staff daily for 10 days beginning 5/15
Editing and Proofreading	Accuracy of spelling, punctuation, grammar	• Costly mistakes • Returned bills • Late payments	10%	Delay in return from original source	Error free	First time	• Debbie S. will create contest with appropriate incentives beginning in second quarter
Drafting Reports	Keep billings current	Improved cash flow with decreased borrowing	10%	• Purpose of many assignments not clear	Same day delivery of all class A reports	Carryover time to complete next day	All staff average will be reduced from 4 hours to 2 hours by 8/1
Telephone and fax use	• Screen calls and fax • Referral to appropriate source	• Save time of manager • Keep customers satisfied	10%	Incoming volume too high—interrupts other work	• Eliminate call backlog • Deliver all fax transmissions within 10 minutes	• Within 2 months • Reduce customer complaints by 50%	Phyllis J. will prepare needs analysis for voice mail system by 10/20

This contract is for the period _____ to _____
                             (mth/day/yr)   (mth/day/yr)

Signed _____

Signed _____ (supervisor)

SAMPLE

PERSONAL PERFORMANCE CONTRACT WORKSHEET

For: **Public Staff Accountant**

Key Result Area	Need	Why Important	How Important %	Potential Obstacles	Performance Targets/Results Expected	Measures Quality/Quantity Time, Cost	Action Plan (Who, What, When)
Productivity	Increase percentage and chargeable bill of chargeable hours	• Improve profit margin • Increase billing rate for adjustments to salary	30%	• Client scheduling problems • Learning curve on new clients	• 90% of hours should be chargeable to client • 90% of hours should be billable to client	• Chargeable hours • Billable hours	• Track charges daily • Set up annual hour plan with supervisor
Timeliness of work	Minimize missed deadlines	• Client's satisfaction depends on service	20%	• Client schedule problems • Busy season/tax season overload	• All work processed in 14 days • Meeting all internal deadlines	• Year end planning budgets • Weekly scheduling analysis	• Review all planning budgets with supervisor
Accuracy of work	Improve quality of work	• Errors reduce productivity • Errors effect timing of jobs	30%	• Distractions in workplace • Failure to establish a method of quality review	• 2% less review points	• Number of review points	• Attend AICPA training class
Communication with client	Get closer to clients	Increase business sold to existing clients	15%	• Creditability • Access to appropriate client personnel	• Contact with all clients per quarter	• Ratio of compliments to problems • Client survey	• Get SAGE training • Attend client meetings with partners
Communication with supervisors	Ease internal hurdles to improve efficiency	Required to best serve clients	5%	• Scheduling conflicts with supervisor	• Daily contact with supervisor • Weekly planning meeting with supervisor	• Number of missed milestones • Percentage of supervisor hours over budget	• Set meeting time with supervisor

This contract is for the period _____ to _____ .
 (mth/day/yr)   (mth/day/yr)

Signed _____

Signed _____
 (supervisor)

SAMPLE

PERSONAL PERFORMANCE CONTRACT WORKSHEET

For: **Customer Service Representative**

Key Result Area	Need	Why Important	How Important %	Potential Obstacles	Performance Targets/Results Expected	Measures Quality/Quantity Time, Cost	Action Plan (Who, What, When)
Respond to customer inquiries	Improve response time to customers by 25%	Must improve customers' perception of our service	40%	Increasing volume of calls and lead time necessary to train service reps	Complete cross-training of all reps by 12/31 and resolve 85% of problems on first call	Percent of problems resolved on first call and average turnaround time on all calls	• Sally/John establish first call, measure by 10/1 • Complete cross-training by 11/1 • Prepare weekly monitoring report by 12/1
Client profitability	80% of time spent with 20% of clients	Must be profitable on all accounts	20%	Price threshold with small accounts and lack of system expertise at some accounts	Identify unprofitable accounts and implement plan to resolve by 12/31	15% profit margin on 90% of accounts and 15% profit margin on all accounts combined	• Publish current profitability report by 10/1 • Implement action plan to correct unprofitable accounts by 10/1 • Regular quarterly reviews by 1/1
Staff development	Train service reps on all products and on more technical aspects of each product	Must resolve client calls more efficiently and reduce customer complaints	10%	Lack of time for internal training and difficulty in simulating live client problems	Each service rep knowledgeable on 50% of products and better technical proficiency	All staff trained on 50% of products and all staff receive technical training	• Assign trainers for internal training by 9/1 • Complete necessary product training by 12/1 • Develop full training schedule for entry-level staff

Key Result Area	Need	Why Important	How Important %	Potential Obstacles	Performance Targets/Results Expected	Measures Quality/Quantity Time, Cost	Action Plan (Who, What, When)
Classroom training	Improve training provided to clients	Improved client satisfaction and fewer service calls	10%	Difficulty in pulling service reps away to spend time on training	Improved training classes and training materials by 12/31	Improved results on class evaluations and better quality of materials for classes	• Laura/Pam develop plan by 9/1 • Classes reviewed and materials developed by 11/1 • Evaluate need to continue project on a regular basis by 1/1
Call escalation	Escalate calls to technical staff person more quickly	Customer service perception	10%	Difficulty in obtaining full commitment from technical and programming staff	Reduce turnaround time on technical calls by 50%	Devote another half-time person and reduce call time by 50%	• Bob assign extra resource by 10/1 • Achieve turnaround time goal by 1/1
Product and sales feedback	Service reps provide better feedback from clients on new product ideas and sales opportunities	Increase sales via continuous product improvement	10%	Concern that someone follows up on the feedback	Improved sales and product features	Number of feedback responses per service rep and some quality measure	• Communicate expectation to all service reps by 10/1 • Monitor results and report results to reps by 1/1

This contract is for the period _____ to _____
                       (mth/day/yr)   (mth/day/yr)

Signed _____

Signed _____
(supervisor)

Personal Performance Contracts

SAMPLE

PERSONAL PERFORMANCE CONTRACT WORKSHEET

For: **Computer Programmer**

Key Result Area	Need	Why Important	How Important %	Potential Obstacles	Performance Targets/Results Expected	Measures Quality/Quantity Time, Cost	Action Plan (Who, What, When)
Software Development	Reduce defect rate	Reduce cost of software development	50%	• Incomplete requirements, design • Low knowledge of testing techniques	• Sign off by programmer on all designs for projects assigned • Review of testing plans with supervisor during first half	• 5% reduction on Q/A testing defects reported by year end • Attendance in Programmer Testing Workshop by 2nd quarter	*Supervisor—* Enrollment in workshop by 2/1 *Supervisor/ Programmer—* Review design walk through process 1/15 *Supervisor—* Schedule time for design walk through for each project per project plan *Programmer—* Attend Workshop by 4/1 *Supervisor—* Review programmer test plans per project
Software Maintenance	Decrease turnaround of reported problem resolution	User productivity is decreasing	25%	• Lack of supporting documentation of problem/software • Time scheduling conflict w/assigned projects	Reduce average # days outstanding of all problems from 12 to 10 by 12/15	• # of problems • # days outstanding • Daily report • Weekly turnaround summary report	*Supervisor—* Allocate time in schedule for maintenance/problem resolution, ongoing *Programmer—* Problem status report, daily *Supervisor—* summary report, every Monday

Key Result Area	Need	Why Important	How Important %	Potential Obstacles	Performance Targets/Results Expected	Measures Quality/Quantity Time, Cost	Action Plan (Who, What, When)
System Resource Utilization	Reduce personal system utilization	Avoid capital expenditure for system upgrade	10%	Missing of project and/or problem resolution dead lines	• Recuce CPU utilization by 10% by 2nd half • Recuce disk utilization by 10% by year end	• % CPU time utilized • % Disk storage utilized	*System operator*—Produce CPU/Disk utilization report, every Monday *Supervisor*—Analyze programmer CPU utilization, by 3/1 *Programmer*—Determine method to reduce CPU utilization, by 4/1 *Supervisor*—Analyze programmer Disk utilization, by 7/1 *Programmer*—Reduce CPU and disk utilization by 10%, by 8/1
Technical Documentation	Too many technical programs are undocumented	Required to maintain user support quality measures	15%	• Time not allocated in project plan • Insuffient technical documentation standards	Complete technical documentation on 100% of new programs developed	• 100% completion of technical documentation • Sign-off on program inspection	*Supervisor*—Review time allocation for documentation, per project *Programmer*—Review technical documentation standards, by 2/1 • Write technical documentation, per schedule

This contract is for the period _____ to _____
                                   (mth/day/yr)   (mth/day/yr)

Signed _____
          (supervisor)

Signed _____

Personal Performance Contracts

SAMPLE

PERSONAL PERFORMANCE CONTRACT WORKSHEET

For: **Restaurant Manager**

Key Result Area	Need	Why Important	How Important %	Potential Obstacles	Performance Targets/Results Expected	Measures Quality/Quantity Time, Cost	Action Plan (Who, What, When)
Food Cost Control	Profits off 7% this quarter	Must meet budget	30%	• Pricing from suppliers • In-restaurant procedures	Reduce food cost by 5% via proper ingredient handling/ordering and usage	• Weekly inventories • P&L statements	*Mgr.*—Retrain staff on portion control by 4/1 • Maintain budgeted inventories by 3/15
Labor Cost Control	Profits off 7% this quarter	Must meet budget	30%	Employee turnover/employee pay increases due	Reduce labor costs by 3% via proper scheduling and labor management	• P&L Statements • Payroll Reports	*Mgr.*—Review screening guides to reduce turnover/training costs by 3/10 • Review labor schedule every Wed. with a Area Mgr. to verify staffing requirements • Eliminate overtime usage by 3/30
Reports	• Monitor progress • Correct problems of late reports and errors	• To ensure that upper management reviews information on time • Government requirements	20%	• Unexpected business in the restaurant	• Daily reports received when due	• Errors within agreed upon limits	*Mgr.*—Schedule 6 hours per week on labor plan beginning 4/1 • Train assistant Mgr. to accurately complete all paperwork in managers absence by 4/10

Key Result Area	Need	Why Important	How Important %	Potential Obstacles	Performance Targets/Results Expected	Measures Quality/Quantity Time, Cost	Action Plan (Who, What, When)
Local Marketing	Increase sales	New competition is encroaching	10%	• Not in budget • No plan in place	2% sales increase via one effective local promotion in place at all times	• Reporting through marketing department • Coupon redemptions	*Mgr.*—Write a marketing plan for the restaurant by 4/1 • Contact Joe in the marketing department for input by 3/20 • Schedule marketing time on weekly labor schedule
Government/ Corporate Policy Compliance	Accuracy in execution of policies/regulations	Avoid lawsuits, fines and penalties	10%	• Poor planning • Complicated regulations	Include policy compliance as 15% bonus factor	• Unscheduled inspections of files and posted materials • Employee questionnaires	*Mgr.*—Review policy manual by 4/1 • Read government regulations for safety, labor, hiring, reporting by 4/5 • Meet with assistant managers by 4/15 to ensure that they understand the procedures • Contact Deb in Human Resources by 3/25 to verify that the information available is current

This contract is for the period _____ to _____ .
                            (mth/day/yr)   (mth/day/yr)

Signed _____
                (supervisor)

Personal Performance Contracts

SAMPLE

PERSONAL PERFORMANCE CONTRACT WORKSHEET

For: **Realtor**

Key Result Area	Need	Why Important	How Important %	Potential Obstacles	Performance Targets/Results Expected	Measures Quality/Quantity Time, Cost	Action Plan (Who, What, When)
Potential Listings	• To increase # of listings each year • To increase average price of listings taken • To increase # of contacts made for potential listings	• # factor in retaining longevity in Real Estate • To increase income without increasing time spent on job	40%	• Quantity of competition • Time restraints • Budget considerations	To increase # of listings each year over last six years	• To increase # of listings by % over previous years • To increase average price of listings taken by % over last 3 years • To increase income by % over last year as result of listings	Personal marketing plan to reflect marketing of higher price listings • To record # of potential lister contacts made monthly charting follow-through • To record % of income increase as results of additional listings sold
Active listings	• Advertising budget • Clerical support • Accountability for actives to foster quicker sale	• To increase % of homes sold • To increase number of homes sold within a 90 day period	30%	• Uncooperative sellers • Advertising coordination • Time restraints • Economic and market factors • Buyer demands	• Increase in % of homes sold within a 90 day period • Increase in number of past sellers who provide repeat business	• % of increase of homes sold within 90 days this year vs. last year • % of increase of past sellers who give me repeat business or referrals over last year • % of average decrease of time on market from last year to this year	• Implement monthly calendar of accountability to sellers • Keep accurate records of time frames in which homes are sold/lost to competition

Personal Performance Contracts

Key Result Area	Need	Why Important	How Important %	Potential Obstacles	Performance Targets/Results Expected	Measures Quality/Quantity Time, Cost	Action Plan (Who, What, When)
Potential sales	• To increase # of sales each year • To increase income as a result of sales closed • To increase # of contacts made for potential sales • To increase conversion rates of potential customers to closed sales	Vital in generating income	25%	• Strong competition • Economic factors • Time restraints • Market inventory	• To increase # of sales annually • To increase average price of home sold annually • To increase income annually as a result of more sales	• To increase # of sales closed by % over last year • To increase income by % over last year as a result of sales closed • To increase conversion rate by % over last year	• To log all contacts made and follow-through • To chart rate of return of income on all sales, ie, time spent, gas to show homes, meals, etc. • Implement personal marketing plan
Follow-through on present sales (before close)	To continue higher % of sales closed than competition	Vital to return business	5%	• Time restraints • Uncooperative attorneys, lenders, etc.	To continue excellent record of sales closed vs. sales recorded	To increase # of buyer referrals by % over last year	• To record all sales that close and/or do not close on time • To implement buyer evaluation program

This contract is for the period _____ to _____
(mth/day/yr)   (mth/day/yr)

Signed _____

Signed _____
(supervisor)

SAMPLE

PERSONAL PERFORMANCE CONTRACT WORKSHEET

For: **Retail Sales Associate**

Key Result Area	Need	Why Important	How Important %	Potential Obstacles	Performance Targets/Results Expected	Measures Quality/Quantity Time, Cost	Action Plan (Who, What, When)
Sales Productivity	To exceed last year sales by 5% to meet store goal	Sales and profits must be improved by 5%	40%	Business trends are relatively flat	All customers must be shown multiple pairs of footwear, be cross sold, and have a "sundry item" presented	Achievement of the 5% above last year in actual dollars sold, pairs per hour, pairs per transaction and sundries also improved by 5%	• Store manager presents goals to salesperson on 2/15 • Salesperson achieves required productivity levels within 30 days 3/15 • Store Manager reviews productivity results and reemphasizes goals quarterly
Customer Service Skills	Achieve and maintain exemplary customer service at all times	Retain current customers and attract new ones	25%	• Unexpected problems on returned goods • Ratio of salespeople to customers in store sometimes causes understaffing	Minimum acceptable rating on all measurements in Customer Service Scale	Achievement of at least 75 on all secret shopping surveys and at least 75 on all customer service comment letters sent to selected refund and regular customers	• Sales Mgr. presents goals to salesperson on 2/15 • Salesperson achieves acceptable results on audits and surveys on a quarterly basis • Store Mgr. reviews results quarterly and goals are adjusted accordingly

Key Result Area	Need	Why Important	How Important %	Potential Obstacles	Performance Targets/Results Expected	Measures Quality/Quantity Time, Cost	Action Plan (Who, What, When)
Non-selling Duties (Stock Work)	Maintain selection via full stock on display	Goods not available can't be sold	25%	Not enough time to restock when sales are heavy	• Salesperson completes daily non-selling tasks assigned • Weekly shipments must be on shelves within 24 hours	Measured daily by store manager	• Store Mgr. will make and review daily assignments with salesperson • Store Mgr. will appraise salesperson's progress quarterly
Attendance	• To be on time and present so that the person puts in the scheduled time • Arrive before shift begins and stay until work is completed	Understaffing leads to lower sales	10%	• Interference of non-work activities • Transportation problems • Number of hours scheduled	100% on time for all scheduled hours	• Time card monitored daily • Below 95% does not qualify for employee discount	• Store Mgr. will set expectations by 2/15 • Salesperson will comply with the schedule assigned • Store Mgr. will review quarterly

This contract is for the period _____ to _____
                             (mth/day/yr)   (mth/day/yr)

Signed _____

Signed _____
            (supervisor)

Personal Performance Contracts

SAMPLE

PERSONAL PERFORMANCE CONTRACT WORKSHEET

For: **Restaurant Server**

Key Result Area	Need	Why Important	How Important %	Potential Obstacles	Performance Targets/Results Expected	Measures Quality/Quantity Time, Cost	Action Plan (Who, What, When)
Customer Service	Repeat business	• High sales • Better tips	30%	Crowded conditions during peak periods	• 90% + inspection rating • 95% + satisfied customers on surveys	Unscheduled inspections, comment cards, customer feedback	*Server*—Commits to a plan for improvement by 2/1 • Review service procedures manual by 2/15
Quality Products	Predictable uniform high quality	Losing customers (down 10% this quarter)	35%	Scheduling difficult due to unpredictable business	• 95% + inspection rating • 100% satisfied customers on surveys	Unscheduled inspections, comment cards, customer feedback	*Server*—Attend product training meeting by 2/10 • Pre-prep all possible products immediately and continuously • Develop a production schedule by 2/20 • Use daily
Home Deliveries	On time per commitment	Competition does it better	25%	Traffic and weather	95% under 30 minute deliveries	Time clocks	*Server*—Fill truck with fuel before each shift • Attend delivery training session by 2/11 • Get shoes that are comfortable for running by 2/20

Key Result Area	Need	Why Important	How Important %	Potential Obstacles	Performance Targets/Results Expected	Measures Quality/Quantity Time, Cost	Action Plan (Who, What, When)
Security/Safety	• Insure safety of employees and customers • Reduce accidents and loss (food and cash)	• Responsibility to workers and customers • Insurance claims are up	10% 100%	Unlocked doors—unrestricted entry to the restaurant	• No accidents • Reduce "shrink" by 20% by 12/1	Workers comp. claims, insurance claims, robberies, unexplained cash and food loss	*Server*—Read safety guidelines by 2/20 and pass test by 3/1 *Manager*—Try new preemployment screening tests by 5/1

This contract is for the period _____ to _____ .
                    (mth/day/yr)   (mth/day/yr)

Signed _____

Signed _____
      (supervisor)

Personal Performance Contracts

CASE #2

NOTE: For a highly regarded book on how to conduct an effective performance appraisal, see page 93.

APPRAISAL =

OBJECTIVE PERFORMANCE EVALUATION

CASE 2: WHAT WOULD YOU DO?

It was seven p.m. and the office had been closed for two hours, but Sue Fleming was still at her desk. She was finishing a report due the next morning. Although she normally enjoyed preparing such reports, she was annoyed with herself for not taking a stronger stand when information for the report was turned in half-finished by Mary Keller, one of her employees. If this had been the only time that Mary had turned in unfinished work Sue would not have been angry. The problem was that Mary did this regularly. On several occasions Sue had to delay completing a design proposal that was Mary's responsibility.

Management textbooks often call Mary's action ''delegating upward'' or ''reverse delegation.'' The first step recommended by a textbook to deal with the problem is to confront the employee. Sue doesn't want to do that. None of Mary's previous supervisors complained about her performance, and Sue doesn't want to call attention to a problem that might somehow be her fault. Besides, she thought, staying late once in a while isn't the end of the world.

A. What effect is the situation likely to have on Sue?

B. What effect is this situation likely to have on Mary?

C. How would you deal with this situation if you were Sue?

D. How would you introduce a PPC to Mary?

Compare your thoughts with those of the author on page 83.

$$\boxed{\text{STEP 3}}$$

COMMIT TO AN ACTION PLAN
TO ACHIEVE RESULTS

Many people hesitate to commit to a plan. They often feel it is not possible to assess what they do because of varied responsibilities and a complex job.

Some jobs <u>are</u> more difficult to assess than others, but every job can be measured. Yet, even with a good measurement system, little is likely to happen unless specific accountability is assigned for each step.

Objectives tell how much progress needs to be made, and where to concentrate. An action plan describes <u>who</u> will do <u>what</u> by <u>when</u>.

A step-by-step method to build a solid action plan is presented on the next five pages.

BUILDING AN ACTION PLAN

An effective Action Plan should:

DESIGNATE who is required to carry the plan to success;

DETAIL what activity or equipment is needed to achieve the planned objectives;

SPECIFY when checkpoints need to be met; and

DETERMINE which alternative courses of action should be available.

Careful preparation is essential if the performance contract is to achieve the results expected. Properly done, a thoughtful action plan will provide these indirect benefits:

1. Time management will improve because:
   - There is agreement on where to concentrate.
   - Low priority activities can be dropped or reassigned.
   - There will be fewer "false starts" or changes in direction.

2. Teamwork will improve because key players have a common game plan;

3. Rate and severity of errors will decrease;

4. There will be fewer excuses because of assigned accountability.

AFTER REVIEWING THE PLANNING FORMAT CAREFULLY, EACH EMPLOYEE SHOULD COMPLETE A FORM SIMILAR TO THE ONE ON THE FACING PAGE. THEN THE COMPLETED FORM SHOULD BE REVIEWED BY THE APPROPRIATE SUPERVISOR/MANAGER.

SAMPLE AHEAD

ACTION PLAN SAMPLE

OBJECTIVES & PLANS OF ACTION	Dept: BUSINESS OFFICE Position: SUPERVISOR	Prepared By:	Date: 2-2-	Page 1 of 1 Pages

OBJECTIVES & RESULTS

(SPECIFIC RESULTS to be accomplished:
WHAT   WHERE
WHEN   and
NET COST-BENEFIT)

HOW (TO ACCOMPLISH IT)	When To Be Done (Schedule)	Who is To Do It (Assgm't)	Approved By	Status & Dates
1. Realign registration procedures.				
A. Prepare procedures and flow charts covering the new system.	2-4	R.S. S.S.	C.Z. W.B.	
B. Train clerks to phase out the preparation of old folders and put new system into effect.	2-15	S.S.	R.S.	
C. Discontinue preparation of old folders—in out-patient registration department.	2-15	S.S.	R.S.	
D. Maintain a file of registration forms—and deliver to all supervisors.	2-14	S.S.	R.S.	
2. Realign the file room procedures.				
A. Prepare procedures and flow charts—covering the file room procedures	2-6	L.A. R.S.	C.Z. W.B.	
B. Train file room staff—in micro-fiche systems and procedures	2-10	L.A.	R.S.	
C. Check bills—for accuracy and completeness.	2-11	L.A.	R.S.	
D. Maintain a file of bills—and deliver to supervisor.	2-10	L.A.	R.S.	
E. Preparation of new folders.	2-14	L.A.	R.S.	

Objective #1 of 5 Weight 25%

WHAT

Develop a micro-fiche system for all itemized bills to eliminate preparation, matching, in-filing, out-filing and microfilming of 4000 records per month

WHEN

To be operational by 3/1

WHERE

At Headquarters

NET COST BENEFIT

Estimated savings of $30,000 p/year

Distribution to:

Reviewed By:

Position:

Dates:

Follow Up:

Write each Objective and Plan of Action on a separate page

Personal Performance Contracts

Without an action plan, goals are merely good intentions. **Action Plans** are necessary to pin down accountability. They determine <u>Who</u> will do <u>What</u> by <u>When</u>.

Following the example on page 51, you should now be ready to prepare an **Action Plan** for one of your highest priority objectives. Use a pencil so you can readily make changes. Be sure to answer these important questions:

–Is the objective really worth accomplishing? Will it make a significant difference when completed?

–Will completing it be cost-effective?

–Do I know the financial impact? Is it significant? Would my boss agree?

–Have the necessary steps been determined? Is the sequence proper?

–Have the right people been informed? Involved?

–Are the deadlines realistic?

–Are the interim checkpoints acceptable?

NOW IT'S YOUR TURN

Write one objective and Plan of Action on this page.

NAME _____

PAGE ____ OF ____

POSITION _____

DATE ____

OBJECTIVES & RESULTS (SPECIFIC RESULTS to be accomplished: WHAT WHEN and WHERE NET COST BENEFIT)	PLAN OF ACTION Sequenced, step-by-step action to take: HOW (TO ACCOMPLISH IT)	When To Be Done (Schedule)	Who is To Do It (Assgm't)	Approved By	Status & Dates
Objective # __ of __ Weight __% WHAT WHEN WHERE NET COST BENEFIT Distribution to:					

Reviewed By:	Position:	Dates:	Follow Up:

Write each Objective and Plan of Action on a separate page

Personal Performance Contracts

To be effective in planning requires follow-up and flexibility. This means you must be prepared to modify or re-direct portions of your plan as situations dictate or conditions change.

To ensure work loads are realistic a <u>SCHEDULE</u> is needed. This is nothing more than a regular means of keeping your plan functioning effectively. You need to:

1. Anticipate the amount of time required to meet deadlines

2. Determine if objectives are being achieved on schedule

3. Personally check any problem that causes a delay

4. Ensure the project deadlines remain realistic, and

5. KEEP EVERYONE INFORMED OF PROGRESS!

SAMPLE AHEAD ⟩

NAME_____

REVIEW/REVISE WORKSHEET

OBJECTIVE NUMBER _____

MONTH	DATE	CHANGES REQUIRED IN OBJECTIVES/PLAN
January	1st Monday	Bid specs not accurate; no input from legal department
February	3rd Monday	Revised bid specs sent on 1/25 (6 days late)
March	3rd Monday	Low bid still $85,000 over projected cost
April	1st Monday	Specs rewritten and approved on 3/20 (35 days late)
May	1st Monday	3 new bidders solicited
May	3rd Monday	New bid accepted ($65,000 under previous low bid)
June	2nd Monday	Contract signed (55 days later than original goal)

PREPARE THE BLANK <u>REVIEW/REVISE</u> <u>WORKSHEET</u> ON THE FACING PAGE FOR EACH OF YOUR KEY OBJECTIVES.

CHECK INDIVIDUAL WORKSHEETS TO SEE IF THEY SUPPORT YOUR PERSONAL PLANNING EFFORTS.

DO IT NOW

NAME_____ *

REVIEW/REVISE WORKSHEET

OBJECTIVE NUMBER _____

MONTH	DATE	CHANGES REQUIRED IN OBJECTIVES/PLAN
January		
February		
March		
April		
May		
June		
July		
August		
September		
October		
November		
December		

*This worksheet may be reproduced without further permission from the publisher.

| STEP 4 |

HOW TO INTRODUCE THE PERSONAL PERFORMANCE CONTRACT

Employees should understand that a Personal Performance Contract, more than any other document, will educate them about how much they are needed. A carefully prepared PPC should emphasize:

- Improving product quality

- Streamlining operations

- Improving customer satisfaction

- Increasing productivity

- Upgrading efficiency

- Cutting down time

- Increasing profits

- Developing markets

- Stimulating morale

or . . .

- Suggesting new ideas on ways trouble can be avoided

PPC's SHOULD MAKE EACH EMPLOYEE FEEL LIKE PART OF A WINNING TEAM

TIPS TO COMPLETE THE PPC

As you prepare to fill out a Personal Performance Contract with your employees, keep these guidelines in mind:

- Plan the meeting carefully

- Establish a friendly "we" atmosphere

- Ask the employee to participate by summarizing what she/he has prepared

- Encourage initiative

- Help employees keep contracts as simple, brief and clear as possible

- Ensure results are measurable

- Get commitments (dates and schedules) from those involved

- Probe to ensure that the objectives and action plans are realistic

- Summarize the expected results of each goal and action plan

- Thank employees for participating and inform them you will be interested in tracking their progress

- Answer any questions

ELIMINATING OBJECTIONS

Often items will surface in a PPC that are likely to bring objections from the person reviewing the plan. When this is anticipated, an "objection-eliminator" worksheet should be prepared. A sample is shown on the facing page.

SAMPLE AHEAD

OBJECTION-ELIMINATOR
WORKSHEET

ITEM IN PPC THAT MAY RAISE QUESTIONS/ OBJECTIONS	SUPPORTING EVIDENCE	BENEFITS	PRESENTATION METHODS
Assign Ed Smith as assistant manager—accounts receivable.	Ed has more than 6 years experience in handling billing procedures (2 with us—4 with a competitor) He spent the last 6 months setting up billing procedures with our computer staff He wants to transfer and his present boss agrees This job would be a logical promotion He should qualify as my replacement within 2 years or he could be promoted to the midwest division	**BENEFITS FOR BOSS** Reduce overtime by 15% (estimated to save $2,300) Eliminate need for outside help at end of each month (estimated to save $7,500) Decrease overdue accounts receivable (Estimated to save $2,800) **BENEFITS FOR COMPANY** Save up to $38,000 per year **BENEFITS FOR CUSTOMERS** Invoices received same time each month Mistakes reduced by 10% Prompt payors will not be subsidizing poor payors	AUDIO VISUALS DOCUMENTS Show time sheets for last 6 months Mgmt. costs resulting from overtime and expenses from help brought in from outside STAFF OTHER Show letters of complaint from customers about late invoices

DO YOU OR YOUR EMPLOYEES HAVE
OBJECTIONS THAT NEED ELIMINATING?

IF SO, USE THE FORM ON THE FACING PAGE.

OBJECTION-ELIMINATOR WORKSHEET*

ITEM IN PPC THAT MAY RAISE QUESTIONS/ OBJECTIONS	SUPPORTING EVIDENCE	BENEFITS	PRESENTATION METHODS
		BENEFITS FOR BOSS	AUDIO
			VISUALS
		BENEFITS FOR COMPANY	DOCUMENTS
		BENEFITS FOR CUSTOMERS	STAFF
			OTHER

*This sheet may be copied without further permission of the publisher.

| STEP 5 | FOLLOWING THROUGH ON PERFORMANCE CONTRACTS |

FOLLOWING THROUGH ON PERFORMANCE CONTRACTS

Nothing is completely predictable in life, and this includes performance contracts. Changes will occur, often with little or no advance warning.

Because of this uncertainty, PPCs need to be monitored on a regular, continuing basis.

Some people may become discouraged if their PPC and plan do not work out exactly as prepared. They forget that it is human to make mistakes and that plans, despite the checkpoints built into them, can fall short of the mark. There is no way to protect against all random events. That is part of the fun and challenge of life.

Therefore, when a PPC strays off-course, an opportunity exists to encourage your employees not only to determine what's wrong, but to develop an action plan of what to do. One way to accomplish this is to ANALYZE all PPCs at least once a quarter.

The facing page provides a simple way to get things back on track.

CHECKPOINT CHARLIE

CHECKPOINTS FOR ACTION

CHECKPOINT	WHAT TO ANALYZE	ACTIONS TO TAKE
Honestly review performance in relation to objectives defined in the performance contract	What was performance like before the PPC was developed? What is performance at this time? What could it be if PPC is fully realized?	Inspect previous performance evaluations. Review current records. Check PPC to see how well present performance measures up to objectives
Look for weaknesses	Check weak areas in relation to existing conditions, and determine who or what is the cause. If outside assistance is needed, who should be told?	Monitor complaints, oversights, mistakes. Evaluate costs in terms of time lost, downtime, waste, etc. Determine key needs that demand satisfaction and resolve them
Keep an eye on time	Where are the time problems? Can they be accommodated within original PPC?	Pinpoint causes. If timelines were not realistic, reset them to reflect reality
Identify management's needs, requirements and wants	What changes have occurred since the PPC was approved? Which activities/objectives in the PPC are currently of greatest importance to the organization?	Maintain strong communication to insure key individuals have current information. Provide avenues for regular feedback from associates
Check the environment	What is new, unusual or different within markets served by your company? What effect do trends and changing patterns have on the PPC under review?	Read appropriate journals to understand conditions in markets served by the company. Track competition to know how they are doing in the same markets. Adjust PPC as required to reflect environment
Determine what action needs to be taken	Organize, initiate and follow through on viable remaining items in PPC.	Revise PPC as required. Prioritize remaining projects to be accomplished. Decide what needs to be done, by whom and when. Assign accountability for results. Set date for next review.

ASSURING TEAMWORK *

Normally a Personal Performance Contract and action plan will involve others. An employee may request your help, or you may see a need for it. That's when a <u>team</u> approach may be the best answer.

Before acting, however, you should first determine:

• Who must be involved?

• Why are they needed?

• What are the critical tasks for each person?

• Does each person know what is expected of him/her?

• Do team members know what is expected of other members?

• Is the team approach consistent with individual PPCs and objectives of the organization?

In situations requiring teamwork neither the extent of the problem nor the need for assistance can be accurately developed into an effective performance contract until the situation has been analyzed. The checklist on the facing page will help you decide how to follow through.

SITUATION ANALYSIS WORKSHEET ⟩

* For an excellent book on Team Building, see Robert Maddux's *Team Building: An Exercise in Leadership* listed on page 93.

SITUATION ANALYSIS WORKSHEET

1. <u>INVESTIGATE</u>

   ☐ What caused the situation?

   ☐ What has been learned about conditions surrounding the situation?

   ☐ Have notes been made of key points?

2. <u>EVALUATE</u>

   ☐ Has essential information been reviewed for accuracy?

   ☐ Have the key factors been isolated?

   ☐ Is there enough information to develop an action plan?

3. <u>RECORD</u>

   ☐ Can a statement be prepared summarizing the problem or situation?

   > What happened?
   >
   > Who or what is affected?
   >
   > Why did the situation develop?
   >
   > How was the situation discovered?

4. <u>TAKE ACTION</u>

   ☐ Have alternatives been prepared or considered?

   ☐ What results are to be achieved (by whom? by when?)

   ☐ What is the extent of any losses?

   ☐ Has a date been established for follow-up review?

With information from a situation analysis worksheet, it should be possible to decide <u>WHO</u> is best qualified to help, and to <u>DETERMINE</u>:

- The type of assistance required.

- The available alternatives.

- The time, materials and people required.

- An estimate of the costs involved.

- How individual PPCs need to be revised to meet the reality of the new situation.

> The opportunity to work with others as part of a team should be a highly rewarding experience. It can enhance personal job skills, and also lead to new approaches which can generate renewed enthusiasm.

TEAMS HELP EVERYONE

BENEFITS OF TEAMWORK

Perhaps the most important benefits of a legitimate team effort are the after-effects. A meeting with the team is an ideal time to review the situation, discuss the tactics used, and assess results that have been achieved. As you analyze the results together, this is an excellent opportunity to:

• Thank team members for what was accomplished.

• Ask where improvements could have been made.

• Identify obstacles that might affect future situations, and discuss alternatives for dealing with them.

• Solicit ideas for new objectives to incorporate into current performance contracts—and those which will be developed in the future.

Another significant advantage of working as a team lies in the increased knowledge and experience for individual team members. When a team approach works well, <u>everyone</u> in an organization benefits.

THE STEP-BY-STEP PROCESS

So far, we have emphasized creating a personal performance contract by deciding on the WHATS, HOWS, and WHENS involved. Now it is time to become very practical. On the next page are 10 simple steps to follow to ensure your PPC and those of your employees are what you want.

TEN-STEP CHECKLIST

CHECK ☑ EACH STEP AS IT IS COMPLETED.

	DOES MY BOSS AGREE?		
	YES	NO	Why not?

☐   1.   Has the necessary information been gathered?   —   —   ——————

☐   2.   Have the expected key results for the job been identified and recorded?   —   —   ——————

☐   3.   Have the greatest needs for each key result area been determined?   —   —   ——————

☐   4.   Do I know why these needs are important and what result is expected for each?   —   —   ——————

☐   5.   Have I ranked the importance of each result expected?   —   —   ——————

☐   6.   Have I identified potential obstacles?   —   —   ——————

☐   7.   Have I determined the most reasonable and realistic performance targets for each key result area?   —   —   ——————

☐   8.   Do I know which measurement assessments are best (quality, quantity, time, cost)?   —   —   ——————

☐   9.   Does my action plan adequately address accountability? (who will do what by when)   —   —   ——————

☐   10.   Have I involved all key people who can affect the outcome?   —   —   ——————

CREATING COMMITMENT

What should the outcome be of a well-written Personal Performance Contract? One immediate benefit should be a commitment to improve productivity.

Some experts believe a major reason for the decline in the "work ethic" is that many employees feel their jobs are boring or even dehumanizing. Others take less pride in what they do because they consider their work unfulfilling.

The Personal Performance Contract can be a major step in overcoming these problems. A thoughtful PPC should get people involved and make them feel they are making an important contribution. Becoming part of the action, and not a piece of machinery, will provide a sense of personal satisfaction.

A well-done Personal Performance Contract will give employees a chance to accomplish more and to do it better. By involving employees, and working with them, it is possible to take advantage of the pride most want to feel for what they are doing. Perhaps most important of all, a good PPC can put enjoyment into what people are paid to do.

What it takes to develop a high quality PPC is COMMITMENT.

TO LEARN HOW A COMMITMENT CAN BE CREATED CHECK THE FACING PAGE.

STEPS TO CREATE JOB COMMITMENT

1. <u>DEVELOP</u>

   - Ensure that commitments are within the capabilities of each person.

   - Provide advice and direction to help structure meaningful commitments for your employees.

   - Set a good personal example by developing a quality Personal Performance Contract with <u>your</u> boss.

2. <u>WEIGH</u>

   - Determine how well the commitments in each PPC address the highest priority needs of the job at this time.

   - Assess how employee commitments support or reinforce those you have made on your PPC.

   - Evalute how realistic the PPC is relative to problems which stand in the way.

3. <u>DISCUSS</u>

   - Provide regular communication with those involved. Construct avenues for feedback.

   - Ensure that commitments of team members are communicated to everyone directly involved.

   - Determine accountability for all commitments.

4. <u>UTILIZE</u>

   - Encourage individuals to be innovative and develop new solutions.

   - Create opportunities to discuss actions taken, as well as obstacles encountered.

   - Analyze all projects or programs in trouble to determine why they are faltering and what can be done to save them.

STEP 6   THE FINAL STEP

Now, it's time to put it all together. First, review the examples on pages 29-45. Then ask those involved to complete a PPC using the blank form on the facing page. Pencil should be used so changes can be made after discussion between you and each employee.

After revision (as often as it takes), a PPC will be ready for implementation when agreement is reached by you and the employee on it and the action plan required to carry it out.

APPLY WHAT YOU HAVE LEARNED

PERSONAL PERFORMANCE CONTRACT WORKSHEET*

FOR _____

NAME

Key Result Area	Need	Why Important	How Important %	Potential Obstacles	Performance Targets/Results Expected	Measures Quality/Quantity Time, Cost	Action Plan (Who, What, When)

Personal Performance Contracts

On the facing page is an example of a completed PPC. Notice that it follows the basic principles provided throughout this book.

–The key result areas are identified

–The objectives are stated clearly in terms of results expected

–Progress measurements are indicated in terms of quantity, quality, time and cost

IT'S SHOWTIME!

SAMPLE PERFORMANCE CONTRACT

Date: _12/1/XX_

Location: _District Office_

_____

To: _John Simpson:_ District Manager _____

From: _Beverly Jones:_ Local Manager _____

Within the period _1/1 — 3/31_ the following will be accomplished:

I Key Result Area _Service Center Expansion_ _____

OBJECTIVE	Date
Open three new suburban service centers in Fairview, Newport and Mapleton and have them open for business by: Total average cost not to exceed previously established budget in each case.	3/15 Fairview 3/31 Newport 3/1 Mapleton

II Key Result Area _Recruiting/Placement_ _____

OBJECTIVE	Date
Select a qualified service manager from within the company for each of above locations. Selection to be completed by:	2/1 Fairview 2/15 Newport 1/15 Mapleton

III Key Result Area _Training_ _____

OBJECTIVE	Date
Train service manager for above new locations. Training content to be developed by: Training content to be approved by District Mgr. by: Training to take place by:	1/5 1/10 3/1 Fairview 3/15 Newport 2/15 Mapleton

You will be kept informed of the progress on each of these objectives at our weekly meetings.

I understand that meeting these objectives will be the most significant factors in my performance evaluation and compensation.

Beverly Jones
Local Manager signature

John Simpson
District Manager signature

YOU CAN DO IT!

PERSONAL PERFORMANCE CONTRACT

Date: _____

Location: _____

_____

To: _____

From: _____

Within the period _____ the following will be accomplished:

I Key Result Area _____

OBJECTIVE	Date

II Key Result Area _____

OBJECTIVE	Date

III Key Result Area _____

OBJECTIVE	Date

You will be kept informed of the progress on each of these objectives at our weekly meetings.

I understand that meeting these objectives will be significant factors in my performance evaluation and compensation.

_____

_____

WHAT HAVE YOU LEARNED?

Now it's time to check on what you have
learned. Answer each of the twenty questions
on the facing page. Answers are on page 82.
Give yourself five points for each correct answer.

MEASURE YOUR PROGRESS

It is time to review your
progress. There are twenty
statements on the facing
page. They are either true
or false. Each correct
answer is worth five points.

READING REVIEW

Please answer each of these questions true or false.

True   False

_____ _____   1. Performance Contracts should deal with the details that you are likely to forget about if not put in writing.

_____ _____   2. Projects which are easily accomplished make the best performance contracts.

_____ _____   3. The first step in preparing a PPC is to set objectives.

_____ _____   4. Accountability is determining who will do what by when

_____ _____   5. Your PPC should concentrate on high priorities which achieve significant results.

_____ _____   6. PPC should be designed exclusively from the point of view of the employee.

_____ _____   7. The key to job success is planned, sustained effort.

_____ _____   8. Your strengths and weaknesses should be discussed with your boss when preparing your PPC.

_____ _____   9. Individual PPCs need not necessarily be related to company goals.

_____ _____   10. It's a good idea to use the PPC to measure every aspect of your job.

_____ _____   11. A key result area is the same as a goal.

_____ _____   12. Progress indicators are ways to measure goals.

_____ _____   13. Possible obstacles should be considered after your PPC has been agreed upon.

_____ _____   14. The PPC should be discussed after projects/objectives are completed.

_____ _____   15. The PPC is best introduced in a memo from the company president.

_____ _____   16. Questions and objections should normally be handled by writing them down and then meeting face-to-face to discuss them.

_____ _____   17. Personal Performance Contracts combine top down direction and bottom-up participation.

_____ _____   18. PPCs should be prepared by you after your boss has decided on the problems you should solve.

_____ _____   19. In performance contracts the whats are more important than the hows.

_____ _____   20. The greatest benefits of PPCs are commitment and results.

ANSWERS TO QUESTIONS ON PAGE 81

1. False   PPCs should be concerned with your most important responsibilities.

2. False   Best results are achieved when extra effort is required.

3. False   Unless we <u>analyze needs</u> first we may set objectives that are meaningless.

4. True

5. True   Don't waste time on "flyspecks."

6. False   <u>Both</u> boss and employee should be involved and agree on the final contract.

7. True   To count on anything else is naive.

8. True   Bosses can't read minds. Worse yet, he/she may guess wrong!

9. False   Any PPC should directly relate to employer expectation and priorities.

10. False   Measurement should be directed toward key result areas and highest priority goals.

11. False   Key result areas are the vital components of your job. It is from these that measurable goals can be constructed.

12. True   They are usually best expressed in terms of quantity, quality, time and cost.

13. False   Anticipation of potential obstacles can sharpen focus and save time.

14. False   Progress should be reported and evaluated regularly.

15. False   To be effective PPCs should be introduced personally by a supervisor.

16. True   Writing tends to focus thinking but "memo wars" without personal contact can make things worse.

17. True   It is this combination which enables managers to function most effectively.

18. False   You should participate at all stages of the PPC.

19. True   We must first be sure we are doing the right things, then concentrate on doing them right.

20. True   Commitment determines persistence. Results (not activities) are what we are paid to achieve.

AUTHOR'S RESPONSE TO CASES

DIFFICULT CHOICES (page 13)

A. A PPC would provide a way to ensure that Joe and Jim were working on the things that most needed to be done. They are drifting because: (1) expectations have not been clearly stated; (2) they are getting by with doing less; (3) Harry is reluctant to deal with them.

   Working together on a PPC will help everyone become aware of the problems, and allow Harry to face the issue of reduced performance.

B. Key Results for Joe as a Production Supervisor should include:
   —production targets and schedules
   —manpower targets and schedules
   —quality control standards
   —cost control targets
   —safety guidelines...etc.

C. As Engineering Supervisor, Jim's key results areas could include:
   —preventive maintenance goals
   —construction contract targets
   —contractor relations guidelines
   —equipment design specifications
   —machine operating standards...etc.

D. Positive results should be shown within six months. Thoughtful PPCs can help. If they do not, Harry Phillips should be removed from his managerial position.

WHAT WOULD YOU DO? (page 47)

A. Sue is likely to find herself doing more and more of Mary's work.

B. Mary may think, "What a great boss I have." Without realizing it, however, she is retarding her own development. She won't grow until she accepts accountability for her work.

C. It is Sue's responsibility as supervisor to take action. She should: (1) stop doing Mary's work; (2) tell her why; (3) help Mary develop a PPC which will incorporate her most important duties in measurable ways; (4) hold Mary to the terms of the contract.

D. We don't know much about Mary's ability, but a PPC should be prepared by Mary (with Sue's help) using the procedures outlined in this book.

VOLUNTARY CONTRACT

Even completing this book may require a personal performance contract of sorts. Why not consider making a contract with a supervisor or friend to complete this book to the best of your ability? If you believe a contract would help, use the form on the facing page.

VOLUNTARY
CONTRACT*

I, _____ , hereby agree
(Your name)

to meet with the individual designated below within

thirty days to discuss my progress toward constructing a

Personal Performance Contract. The purpose of this meeting

will be to *review* areas of strength and establish action steps for

areas where improvement may still be required.

_____
Signature

I agree to meet with the above individual on

_____
Month   *Date*   *Time*

at the following location.

_____

_____
Signature

*The purpose of this agreement is to motivate you to incorporate
concepts and techniques of this program into your daily
activities. It also provides a degree of accountability between
you and the person you select to sign the agreement.

NOTES

FOR OTHER FIFTY-MINUTE SELF-STUDY BOOKS
SEE THE BACK OF THIS BOOK.

NOTES

FOR OTHER FIFTY-MINUTE SELF-STUDY BOOKS
SEE THE BACK OF THIS BOOK.

NOTES

FOR OTHER FIFTY-MINUTE SELF-STUDY BOOKS
SEE THE BACK OF THIS BOOK.

NOTES

FOR OTHER FIFTY-MINUTE SELF-STUDY BOOKS
SEE THE BACK OF THIS BOOK.

FOR OTHER FIFTY-MINUTE SELF-STUDY BOOKS
SEE THE BACK OF THIS BOOK.

NOTES

FOR OTHER FIFTY-MINUTE SELF-STUDY BOOKS
SEE THE BACK OF THIS BOOK.

We hope you enjoyed this book. If so, we have good news for you. This title is part of the best-selling *FIFTY-MINUTE*™ *Series* of books. All *Series* books are similar in size and identical in price. Several are supported with training videos (identified by the symbol ❷ next to the title).

FIFTY-MINUTE Books and Videos are available from your distributor. A free catalog is available upon request from Crisp Publications, Inc., 1200 Hamilton Court, Menlo Park, California 94025.

FIFTY-MINUTE Series Books & Videos organized by general subject area.

Management Training:

Management Training (continued):

Personal Improvement:

Human Resources & Wellness: